A NOTE TO PARENTS AND TEACHERS

Discovery Readers are nonfiction books designed for the beginning reader. Each Discovery Reader is filled with informative text, short sentences, and colorful and whimsical illustrations.

Discovery Readers make nonfiction subjects fun and historical subjects come alive. But nonfiction stories must use some words that cannot be changed for easier ones. For this reason, we encourage you to help the child with the short vocabulary list below before he or she begins the book. Learning these words will make reading the story easier.

VOCABULARY LIST

February	Martha
George	Custis
Washington	America
Virginia	Declaration
Lawrence	Independence
Mount	Congress
Vernon	Revolutionary
French	United
Indian	States

ISBN 0-8249-5505-6

Published by Ideals Children's Books
An imprint of Ideals Publications
A division of Guideposts
535 Metroplex Drive, Suite 250
Nashville, Tennessee 37211

R.L. 2.5 Spache

Text copyright © 2005 by Ideals Publications
Art copyright © 2005 by Stephanie McFetridge Britt

Library of Congress Cataloging-in-Publication Data

Pingry, Patricia A., date.
  Discover George Washington : soldier, farmer, president / Patricia A. Pingry ; illustrated by Stephanie McFetridge Britt.
      p. cm. — (Discovery readers)
  Includes bibliographical references and index.
  ISBN 0-8249-5505-6 (alk. paper)
  1. Washington, George, 1732-1799—Juvenile literature. 2. Presidents—United States—Biography—Juvenile literature. I. Britt, Stephanie, ill. II. Title. III. Series.
  E312.66.P547 2005
  973.4'1'092—dc22

2005003699

Designed by Jenny Eber Hancock

Printed in Italy by LEGO

10 9 8 7 6 5 4 3 2 1

Discover
GEORGE
WASHINGTON

SOLDIER • FARMER • PRESIDENT

WRITTEN BY PATRICIA A. PINGRY

ILLUSTRATED BY STEPHANIE MCFETRIDGE BRITT

ideals children's books.
Nashville, Tennessee

On February 22,
we remember the birthday
of George Washington.

We call him the
"father of our country."

George was born
on a farm in
Virginia in 1732.

There is a story that
young George chopped
down a cherry tree.

He said to his father,
"I cannot tell a lie.
I chopped down
your cherry tree."

That story is not true.
But George always
told the truth.

George helped his
father on the farm.

But George wanted
to be in the army
just like his half
brother Lawrence.

George liked to visit
Lawrence at Mount Vernon.

Lawrence helped George
study for the army.

He studied math and
learned to survey land.

At sixteen, George
was hired to survey land
in the Virginia mountains.

George camped out.
He learned to take
care of himself.

At twenty-one,
George joined the army.
He led troops in the
French and Indian War.

When the war was over,
George went home to
Mount Vernon.

George became a farmer.

He read books about farming.

He studied plants.

Every day George rode
around his farm.
George was a good farmer.

One day George met
a young widow, Martha Custis.
She had two children.
George liked them
all very much.

The next day, he went
to see them again.
He asked Martha
to be his wife.

George was a good stepfather.
He was happy at home.
But his country needed him.

On July 4, 1776,
America signed the
Declaration of Independence.

Congress named George general.
This was his childhood dream.
He would lead an army.

George had a uniform made.
But many of his soldiers
did not have uniforms.

Some men did not have shoes.
They did not have guns or bullets.

George wrote to Congress.
He asked them to
send guns and bullets.

He asked for blankets
and tents and uniforms.
He asked for more shoes.

America was fighting the
Revolutionary War.
George led his army
for six years. In 1781,
George won the war.

Americans thought that
George was the
best general ever.
They thought George
was the best American ever!

In 1789, George was
elected the first president
of the United States.

Martha became the first,
first lady. George was
a very good president.

But after eight years
George and Martha were tired.
They wanted to go
home to Mount Vernon.

Many Americans came
to see the first president.
George and Martha always
had company for dinner.

The new capital of
the United States
was named Washington
to honor George.

Americans built a tall
monument to honor George.
They put his picture
on the one-dollar bill
and on the quarter.

We remember George
as our first president,
a good farmer,
and a brave soldier.